FHM PRESENTS...

THE LITTLE BOOK OF TRUE STORIES

D0273060

THIS IS A CARLTON BOOK

Text copyright © Emap Elan Network 2002, 2004
Design copyright © Carlton Books Limited 2004

This edition published by Carlton Books Limited 2004
20 Mortimer Street
London W1T 3JW

A CIP catalogue record for this book is available from
the British Library.

ISBN 1 84442 709 9

Printed in Singapore

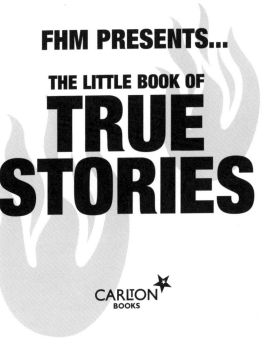

FHM PRESENTS...

THE LITTLE BOOK OF
TRUE
STORIES

CARLTON
BOOKS

Thanks to FHM's readers for all their true stories

www.fhm.com

Dog goes airborne

Army ejects terrier

This happened when I was a young gunner working in Canada, a few years ago. I was operating a Challenger Battle Tank on a live firing exercise one afternoon when we were told by our commanding officer to expect a visit from a high-powered general, and that best behaviour was required. After a few hours of live firing, the order came through to cease fire, and the tanks rumbled out of the greenery to form a neat line for the General's arrival. He arrived by helicopter and, with a small white Scottish terrier under his arm, swiftly made his way along the tanks introducing himself to everyone. When he reached our tank he clambered aboard for a quick look around, patted us

FHM

all on the back, said, 'Right ho, chaps,' climbed off the machine and walked back to his helicopter to get an aerial view of the tanks firing their guns at predetermined targets. As we advanced into position I saw my first target and shouted up to the loader to arm the gun. As he stuck his hand in the charge bag however, he suddenly withdrew it with a loud 'Ouch,' and I turned to see the General's dog with its teeth clamped to the hand of the burly Irish gunner. Angry beyond belief, the gunner suddenly pushed the dog into the barrel of the 120mm gun, slammed the breach closed, looked at me and bellowed 'Fire!' In the heat of the moment I nodded grimly and pulled the trigger; the slobbering canine left our Challenger at mach three, and the spotters radioed through that the General was impressed by our accuracy.

Royal takes charge

Oil worker offends inbred

In the Seventies I was working out in the North Sea on the Claymore Alpha Oil rig. One day we were notified of an impending visit from Prince Charles, and the guy in charge of the deck, a Canadian and staunch Royalist ran us ragged for weeks, taking us through the landing drill over a dozen times. Once the helicopter had landed, the heli-crew would have to wait for the pilot to switch off a flashing red light under the fuselage before they could open the doors. The big day came and it was a scorcher – beautiful sunshine and not a breath of wind. The RAF Sea King appeared and made a perfect touchdown, but although the engines started to slow, the fuselage warning light kept flashing. We waited and waited and then, realising that his drill was starting to fall apart, the Canadian began gesturing to the pilot to turn the light off. He pointed under the aircraft and twirled his fingers frantically, but the confused pilot shrugged his shoulders and shook his head. Furious, the Canadian grabbed the radio and yelled into it, 'Turn off your fucking red light so we can approach your fucking aircraft, you goddam fucking idiot!' The pilot gave an immediate thumbs up and the light went out. He then slowly removed his sunglasses and pulled off his helmet: Prince Charles had opted to fly the helicopter himself that day.

Blind man betrayed

Hospital humiliation for injured worker

I am a self-employed joiner who works away from home, and the following disaster happened to me last year when I was working at a hotel complex in London. I was using an angle-grinder and had a slight accident with a grinding disc. The disc shattered and left a really nasty gash just above my eye, an injury which needed 20 stitches. On the way to the hospital the ambulance medic bandaged both of my eyes shut and told me not to try to open them as this could result in more damage to my eye. After waiting on a hospital bed for over two hours I told my mate, who had come along to give me moral support, that I needed a pee, and he agreed to guide me to the loo. We walked aimlessly around the corridors for several minutes until I was really desperate. Finally, we walked through some doors and my friend positioned me in front of the bowl. I pulled out my cock and sighed, letting the hot gushing stream hit the pan. In seconds I heard howls of laughter and felt a hand on my arm. Then a woman's voice calmly asked me if I would mind not peeing in the wastepaper basket of the outpatient's department. My friend had calmly let me get my todger out in full view of over 20 other patients.

Orderly confuses paste

OAP's foot & mouth mix-up

Many years ago I worked as a hospital orderly looking after elderly, senile patients. One particular woman didn't need much looking after, but understanding any of her requests was tricky due to her severe speech impediment, coupled with the fact that she wore cheap, ill-fitting dentures. One day, I decided to help her out by giving these stained gnashers a good clean, so I gently teased them from her chops and gave them a thorough scrub in the sink. I was proud to see that they looked absolutely gleaming when I had finished, and when I jammed them back in she had a true, gleaming, Hollywood smile. As I set about tidying the rest of the room, however, she suddenly started rolling

around the bed and whimpering. There was also blood streaming out of her gob. Racing over, I grabbed her head, whipped out her dentures and dragged her over to the sink to wash her mouth out. It was only as the old dear was spitting down the drain that I saw the words 'Fungal Foot Cream' printed across what I had supposed to be the toothpaste tube.

Patient forgets amputations

Slippers elude searcher

Many years ago, I worked as an orderly in a local hospital. Although the sight of blood didn't bother me, I could never come to terms with the geriatric ward, where the old timers would continually cast aside blankets, offering me a display of their saggy breasts and greying, dilapidated pubic thatches. To make matters worse, one particularly senile woman mistook me for a wartime spiv, and demanded nylon stockings and bacon whenever I passed. Naturally I always ignored her, but one morning she changed her patter and asked me to fetch her slippers from under the bed. I got down on my knees and looked, but when I explained that they weren't there, she went berserk, shouting, 'What's wrong with you? Why can't you see them?', which was enough to convince me I simply wasn't looking hard enough. Just as it was getting to the stage where I was lifting the bed to look in the corners, the duty nurse tapped me on the shoulder and asked me what I was doing. When I explained I was hunting for the woman's slippers, she simply shook her head and through stifled laughter pointed at a gap in the bed – the precise gap where the old bat's legs should have been.

Word mix-up

Policeman makes a big mistake

As a fresh-faced member of the Metropolitan Police Force, I was once asked to deal with a case of an old Jewish lady who had tragically attempted to take her own life. My partner at the time was an officer with numerous years of experience, and when we arrived at the hospital he propped himself up outside the nurses' rest area and informed me that I would be conducting the interviews. But while he stood there with his chest puffed out, the distraught daughter of the Jewish lady walked up and proceeded to embark on a long tale of suffering and pain, describing in great detail her mother's third suicide attempt. Evidently my partner's concentration had been entirely focused on the young girls in uniform, because he suddenly leant forward and, with as much sincerity as he could muster, boomed, 'Yes – it's tragic, isn't it? It almost makes you believe there's a real case for genocide.' We all stopped what we were doing and a stunned silence followed, before the daughter managed, 'You mean euthanasia, surely?' Realizing his blunder, my colleague nodded, then silently shuffled out of the room, to spend the rest of the afternoon sitting shamefaced in the patrol car.

Road sign no use

Squaddie loses way

This story dates back to when I worked at a parachute-training unit in Germany. We had a foreign skydiving team training with us, and at the end of their stay one of the lads was tasked with driving them to Hanover airport for their flight home. It was a three-hour round trip, and after six hours we started to worry. A quick call to the airport confirmed that he had dropped the team off, so we knew he was somewhere on the road back. Then the phone rang, and a rather panicky squaddie explained that he was lost and had run out of diesel for the van. To make matters worse, he only had one Deutschmark for the phone, and the pips were starting to go. Thinking quickly, we asked

FHM

him if he could see any street signs to indicate his position. There was a brief pause, and then he excitedly replied 'I can see a sign for Rollsplitt. Oh thank God, I'm in Rollsplitt…' before getting cut off. It sounded familiar, but none of us could place it, so we asked our German accountant. 'Rollsplitt?' he asked, completely deadpan, 'but that means loose chippings.'

Engineer inspects firearm

Spud gun fun goes awry

Several years ago I worked night shifts as an electrical maintenance engineer. To pass the time, the team started to devise stupid ways of producing the loudest noise possible. The best technique was to place a mixture of oxygen and acetylene welding gas into a crisp packet, and light it at arm's length, but I developed the idea and came up with 'The Spud Cannon'. Basically a steel pipe with two gas taps and a spark plug, the cannon's power was breathtaking, and could easily put a King Edward clear over the horizon. All was well, until someone stuffed in a soggy tea bag, soaking the spark plug. I loaded and reloaded several times, but to no avail. It was then I made a

critical error and ignored the rule, 'never look down the barrel of a gun'. Peering in to see if a spark was being produced, I pulled the trigger. There was a deafening noise, I went blind, and for a split second I thought I had blown my face off. When I got to a mirror, I realized I had singed my eyebrows and hair, huge pieces of rust from the pipe were embedded in my bleeding nose, and red welts showed where bits of tea leaf had peppered me.

Alcoholic acts deceased

Helpful copper causes anguish

While on duty in the East Midlands, I was sent to an address following a report that the owner of the house had died. The tip had come from a well-known wino, who claimed that he had popped around to his mate's house and found him dead. Unable to stay in the house with the body, he said that he would wait outside the premises until I arrived. When I got there, a crowd of concerned locals, including the deceased's family were standing around, but the wino was nowhere to be seen. The door was firmly locked, but I could see that the upstairs window was ajar, and as everyone was becoming increasingly agitated, I called the fire brigade. Some time later, with a large audience, including six firemen, I ascended the ladder. When I got to the window I could see the body on the sofa, tongue hanging out, and lifeless. But as I opened the window and climbed in he sat bolt upright and looked straight at me. Excitedly I stuck my head out the window and shouted, 'He's alive.' Oh how the family members cried, and the firemen cheered, as they all waved happily at me. And then I felt a tap on the shoulder. 'I suppose you've come for the dead guy in the bedroom,' the wino said. Sheepishly I stuck my head back out and said, 'Actually, he is dead. Sorry.'

In-flight terror

Pilots get locked out

While on a flight across China to take up a post with a minerals exploration company, I was too busy enjoying the spectacular view to bother too much about the slapdash standard of service. It wasn't until a stewardess entered the cockpit shouting at the top of her voice that I realized this was no ordinary flight. After a bit of a barney on the flight deck, she emerged, followed by the co-pilot, and they carried on their heated discussion in front of the passengers. When they'd finished, the co-pilot turned to go back into his cabin, only to realize that the door had jammed. After much rattling, shaking and knocking, the captain came out to demand what was going on.

He stepped out of the cockpit and closed the door behind him in order to deliver a stern lecture to his subordinates. It was only when they tried to open the door again that they realized it had jammed once more. This time, there was no-one left on the flight deck to open the door from the inside, and the captain, his co-pilot and the stewardess were getting more and more frantic as the door wouldn't budge. The passengers were also going mad, and it wasn't until someone found an emergency axe that they chopped down the door and regained the cockpit. For the rest of the flight, we could see the two embarrassed pilots through the splintered hole in their door, glaring at each other like mortal enemies.

Officer's mess

Swedes tempt frisky cop

While performing my duties as an Edinburgh police officer, my partner Colin and I had reason to stop a motorist, who was driving somewhat erratically. As I got out of the car to talk to him, two healthy young blondes started chatting to Colin, who was still sitting in the passenger seat. I spoke to the motorist, decided that he had been drinking, and asked him to accompany me back to the squad car. As he climbed into the back seat I couldn't help but notice that Colin had now exited the vehicle, was flirting like crazy with the giggling blondes, and was even showing them his handcuffs. I got in beside the worried motorist, prepared the breathalyser for the breath test, and put on the sternest face possible to read Section Six of the Road Traffic Act. However, no sooner had I uttered the words 'Now then, sir' when Colin dived into the front seat, slammed the door shut, turned to the pair of us and said: 'She's Swedish, and says if we give her and her a friend a lift up the road, she'll suck my cock!' We stared at Colin's beaming face in stunned silence, until the police radio suddenly garbled a message. In a huge fit of laughter I told the motorist that we had an urgent call to attend and he was free to go. His bemused face, as he stood in the middle of the road and watched us roar off, will stick in my mind for ever.

Fast tracks

Squaddies take up race

While serving out in Africa many years ago as a regular in the army, a mate of mine, Joe, found himself sitting on the roof of an old Bedford bus, heading into the local town with the rest of his mates for what promised to be an almighty piss-up. As they hurtled down the dusty road, a great cheer suddenly went up from the front of the bus as it pulled out and began to slowly overtake a ramshackle pick-up truck. The little pick-up was being driven by an African family, and they were loving the attention, smiling and waving and doing their best to get a race going as the drunken squaddies slowly rumbled past. What was really making the boys laugh, however, was the grandmother. Due to the severe lack of space, she had been rolled up in a dirty red carpet and strapped to the roof rack. With only her wrinkled face visible, she jutted out about five foot in front of the truck, leading the charge with grim determination. Then, as Joe's bus inevitably pulled away, she emitted a banshee-like wail as she disappeared in a cloud of dust and diesel.

Local poultry

Sailors regret chicken dinner

In 1995 I was in the Royal Navy serving onboard HMS Southampton in the West Indies. Visiting the islands in the Caribbean while doing our country's bit for the counter-drugs operation, one of our stops was the island of Montserrat. Our stay took the usual form of getting ashore and downing as much low-priced white rum as possible. Every bar seemed to offer much the same as the last: cheap booze and identical menus containing 'mountain chicken' and chips. After the fourth, we were starving and being adventurous we all opted for the chicken. When it came there only seemed to be chicken legs. The barman explained that because of the mountainous island, the legs of the mountain chicken were very big and the best part, so we tucked in. Two months later, when the island's volcano erupted, we were called back to aid in the disaster relief operation. We were erecting tents for the islanders to wait out the eruptions when, during a break, the biggest bullfrog we had ever seen – as big as a small dog – bounded across the field. We all laughed as this enormous amphibian hopped by. The laughter soon stopped when an old woman who was chasing it shouted, 'Hey, stop that mountain chicken!'

Early shout

Fireman suffers slow burn

I'm a member of the fire service, and recently had to have a vasectomy. The night before the operation I received a phone call from a Nurse Smithers, confirming my appointment and reminding me to bring a pair of tight underpants and fresh urine and sperm samples. The urine sample did not prove a problem, but the sperm donation reduced my wife to hysterics as I struggled nervously – the morning of the operation – to beat my non-responsive member into action. Finally my pathetic secretions were bottled, and off I went to hospital. The operation was a success, but I was slightly annoyed when the medical staff ignored my hard-won samples – although by the time my wife arrived to take me home I was past caring. It was only when I returned to work that I discovered that 'Nurse Smithers' was in fact a work colleague, and that, during the 09:00hr parade – just about the time I was beating my floppy member into oblivion – a full squad of 22 firefighters had performed a mass groan of sympathy.

Suspect device

Soldier's heroics backfire

I am presently on a tour with a rifle company, serving
in Belfast. While out and about a few months ago I
noticed something which I thought required my
expertise as a Unit Search Advisor: near a large tree a
plank had been put across a hole in the ground, and
leaves had been scattered over the board in an
attempt at concealment. I went over with a member of
my unit. We pulled the plank clear, and bingo! I found
a small box, eight inches by four inches, the same size
as a TPU (timer power unit) – a component in many of
the terrorist devices used in the province. On closer
inspection I saw that the box was made of cardboard,
and I gingerly removed the lid. Inside, I saw a package

wrapped in a handkerchief, with what looked like a piece of string sticking out of it. I decided to uncover the device, and at this point my company commander suggested we call in the experts. I resisted, seeking the glory for myself. I gently lifted the string and the handkerchief fell away. At that moment, my place in battalion legend became secure: the string was in fact a tail. In the torch beams we stared at a dead hamster, ruthlessly plucked from its lovingly constructed grave.

Deterrent misused

Bobby belts enraged beast

This story dates back to when I was a police probationer, being shown the ropes by an experienced copper called Baz. We were on routine patrol one night when a call was received of 'intruders on the premises' at a local breaker's yard. Baz was all too aware that the place was guarded by a vicious Rottweiler named Sid, so when we arrived he pulled out his trusty Halon fire extinguisher – an exceptional deterrent when sprayed into an animal's eyes. Our shift sergeant duly arrived and confidently led the way into the dark yard. No sooner had we rounded the first corner when the slavering Sid confronted us, baring his teeth and growling with intent. Then he charged us. Rather than run however, the sergeant decided he was Crocodile Dundee and attempted to out-stare the beast. It didn't work, and when Sid was a mere 15 metres away, Baz grabbed the extinguisher and yelled 'Here, sarge, use this!' The sarge nodded grimly, took it and swung it high over his head, bringing it down on the leaping mutt's cranium with a massive thud, killing it outright. 'Not quite what I had in mind, sarge,' was all a bemused Baz could say.

Welcome to Bosnia

Copper's 'friendly' fire

My mate Norm is a copper who often had to work the night shift. To relieve the tedium, the bobbies devised a game: cowboys and Indians. They would stalk each other in the dead of night, while the town slept peacefully. Norm was a cowboy, but, being a bit slow, he was often subjected to vicious barrages of arrows. So, in order to exact revenge, he bought himself a blank-firing pistol. However, after two weeks of patrolling his territory, without seeing any Injuns, he began to wonder whether he was ever going to christen his peacemaker. One evening, having stopped in a doorway for a break, he could suddenly hear approaching footsteps. 'Ha!' thought Norm. 'This has got to be an Indian.' Out came the peacemaker and, with a devilish glint in his eye, Norm waited. Then, as the adrenalin pumped and the sweat dripped off his brow, Norm jumped into the street and shot at the Indian. But, to his horror, the victim was not an Indian. Norm vividly recalls watching his gun smoking, while an innocent member of the public lay sprawled on the floor, suffering a severe shock and involuntary urination and defecation.

Bucket contains surprise

Workers get unwelcome shower

Last summer I found myself refurbishing The King Solomon Hotel in Israel with another Brit in an attempt to earn enough cash for a ticket home. Our job was to rip the tables, mirrors and beds out of the rooms and throw them 14 floors down into the skips below. In one such room my fellow worker discovered a sealed 20-litre bucket of shit, which had been used by previous labourers as a toilet. Not knowing what to do with it, he hurled it over the edge, and we watched it plummet down to the ground. To our surprise, it remained intact. We forgot about it until four days later, when the whole team was led out to the courtyard to empty the skips. Two lads climbed up onto the piles and started throwing rubbish down to us – which was when, to my horror, I noticed a familiar-looking bucket soaring through the air. With no time to offer a warning, I bailed out of the way as the bucket hit with an explosion of spicy gases, spraying everyone with a heady cocktail of human faeces and urine. The result was a spontaneous vomiting session, as grown men puked until they could no longer stand.

Wheelchair deception

Guide embarrasses punter

About five years ago I worked as a backstage tour guide for a well-known television station. Part of the tour included an explanation of the intricate details of the blue screen – where anything coloured blue fails to show up on camera. To do this properly, my group had to climb a near-vertical ramp and take their places in fitted seats, from where they could see themselves embarking on a magical journey via the screen in front of them. On this particular occasion I had a middle-aged lady in a wheelchair on my tour, who for obvious reasons could not get up into a chair, so I placed her at the front so that she could still see herself and enjoy the show. As the ride began, I explained that if

FHM

anyone was actually wearing an item of blue clothing, it would look as if it had disappeared. Trying not to leave anybody out, I pointed at the lady at the front and said, 'Ladies and gentlemen, if you look you will see that this lady is obviously wearing blue trousers, as you cannot see her legs.' To my utter horror, she slowly turned towards me and replied, 'Actually, I don't have any legs.'

Restaurant urination disaster

Closing time cock-up

About ten years ago, while serving with the RAF, a few of my fellow airmen and I were on exercise near a village in North Wales. The end-of-exercise binge coincided with FA Cup final Saturday and a large contingent of RAF lads descended on the local hostelry. The landlord agreed to keep the pub open all day, only closing between 5pm and 6pm to clean up and replenish the shelves. As soon as he had closed the door on us at 5pm I felt the desperate need to urinate. The village was deserted and without public conveniences. I found an alleyway, which had a brick wall on one side and a large shop window on the other, which seemed to be painted from the inside

FHM

with black paint. I was blissfully engaged in the most satisfying pee I had ever had when I was accosted in mid-stream by a burly Welshman who, in mixed English and Welsh, accused me of exposing myself and peeing against the window of a restaurant. Apparently, although I couldn't see in, 30 or 40 people, including a local landowner with his daughter and prospective son-in-law, and a contingent of nuns from a nearby convent, could see out! The worst part of the whole affair was that after the local police were called and gave me a good telling off in front of the locals, I was assured that no further action would be taken. On my return to base, though, I found that a summons had been served on my CO. I paid a £20 fine and lost several years seniority in rank.

Workman stuck

Hound gets hots for gasman

While working some time ago as a gasman in Manchester, I received a call on my radio asking me to assist another workman in the area. When I arrived at the house, I found the carpet rolled back and the head of my friend sticking out through a lifted floorboard. When saw me, he shouted that he needed some extra pipe and nodded his head in the direction of his van. Unfortunately, the subsequent motion of his long hair and beard attracted the attention of the customer's poodle, who embarked on a sexual assault of such ferocity on my friend's head that his unthinking reaction was to try to stand up, jamming himself between the floorboards. With one paw covering his eye and another stuffed in his mouth, his furious head-shaking only served to excite the eager pooch to ever more energetic arousal: it was jerking away at breakneck speed, eyes crossed and tongue flapping wildly. Fortunately, just as it looked as if the dog was about to come in my mate's ear, the poodle's owner came flying in and booted the dog across the room. These days, my mate sports a crew-cut.

Car lads hoard pants

About a year ago, I sold used cars for a city-centre
dealer. We worked out of two huge Portakabins, one
nice and clean for the customers, the other a 'snake
pit' for eight salesmen. It was horrific, full of dirty
magazines, men swearing and filthy mugs. Our
favourite item, however, was what we called the
Trophy Tree. Basically, whenever we delivered a car,
we would ask to use the toilet. While in there, a quick
root through the laundry basket was undertaken, and
the dirtiest pair of knickers stolen. The offending item
then went on the tree, points being awarded on a
scale of sauciness, amount of material soiled and sex-
appeal of the owner. One day one of the lads was

lounging around in our private cabin when the door flew open and in walked a customer. 'What's that?' laughed the bloke at the door, pointing at our tree. 'It's a trophy tree,' my friend Mark answered sheepishly, explaining that the boys brought in knickers from the girls they had scored with over the weekend. The customer thought it was brilliant and recounted bawdy tales of his youth. As he left he pointed at a nasty grey pair and sighed, 'That's all my missus wears these days, though.' We never heard from him again, but the awful fact is that they were the dirty grots of his beloved wife. Mark had stolen them the previous week.

Jungle boogie

Squaddie vs reptile

During a break from patrolling the jungle in Belize, my platoon stopped to enjoy a quiet afternoon of drinking and sunbathing. Spotting a turtle in a storm drain, we brought it over for a closer look. Its immediate response was to extend its neck slightly and open its beak in a gesture designed to frighten away pissed-up squaddies. While most of us could recognize an angry snapper turtle when we saw one, one guy – Tam – was blissfully ignorant, and we cringed as he held the livid creature at waist level, took his member out and laughingly demanded oral sex. Suddenly there was a blur of movement – the snapper had stretched out and clamped down on the idiot's meat and potatoes. We were then treated to the sight of a screaming Tam, charging through the jungle with an angry green turtle dangling from his cock. Amazingly, both parties survived, but we never did manage to ascertain who emerged most traumatized.

Plumbing gaff

Old boiler gets a shock

While relaxing after an enormous roast dinner one Sunday afternoon, the telephone rang. I am a plumber, so it is not unusual for me to get emergency call-outs, and sure enough, it was one of my elderly and more snooty customers. Apparently, her boiler was making unusual noises and she was worried it might explode. So, with much regret at having had my day off interrupted, I agreed to go over to her house. She met me at the front door and I asked her where the boiler was located. She informed me it was a wall-mounted boiler in the kitchen, over the worktop, so I walked through to the kitchen, thinking the old lady had stayed in the hall. In the kitchen, I climbed onto the worktop to inspect the boiler, but as I did so, I let out a fart of epic proportions. I was mortified, therefore, to find the lady of the house standing behind me with a look of contempt on her face. Thinking it would be too rude and obvious to simply apologize, all I could say was, 'Is the boiler making a noise similar to that?'

Financial farrago

Sleepy bank wakes up

A few years ago, I was working in Southampton for a national bank as a trainee manager. Every couple of months or so, my boss would poke his head out of his office and despatch one of his boys off to some remote branch for 'a taste of the real world'. That's how, one rainy October morning, I found myself standing on a deserted railway platform far away in the Cheshire countryside. After wandering through the peaceful hamlet, I located the branch of my bank, where I was royally greeted and shown into a huge room – the regular manager was on holiday, and I could use his office. The assistant manager saw me settled in, then shut the door, screening off from my sight the bumpkins queuing up to cash their EC subsidies. I unpacked my briefcase, shuffled a few papers, and realized I didn't have a clue what to do next. Glancing around, I found a nice big button under an old copy of the FT. 'Tea!' I thought, and buzzed the assistant. I couldn't hear a thing, so I gave the buzzer another good old push. But my daydreaming was interrupted by a banshee wail. Rushing out, I was greeted by the sight of a middle-aged lady teller collapsed in tears in the street. I'd been pressing the silent alarm, and the poor woman I'd terrified had just been transferred to the bucolic village. She had been held up at the Wolverhampton branch two weeks earlier.

Fireman framed

Armed robber innocent

It was my third day as a fireman. My station was in two parts – one for the appliances, the other for tools and admin. My boss asked me if I could take some gear to be serviced at the second part of the station. I was wearing full kit – boots, orange trousers and black donkey jacket and they loaded me up with breathing apparatus (helmet on, as my hands were full). One of the guys handed me an old pickaxe handle which needed reheading. As I walked out of the station our office clerk handed me a deposit envelope, asking me to drop it into the bank on the way past. At the bank I attracted a few odd looks as I waited in the queue. Eventually I gave a cashier the envelope. She asked me to wait for my receipt. I leaned on the counter, leafed through a brochure and waited. And waited. Thinking she was taking her time, I looked up and she'd gone. Well, not exactly gone, but standing with the rest of the staff in a far corner looking past me at the bank's entrance. I followed her gaze and nearly shit myself. An armed policeman in a crouched firing position told me very firmly to drop the axe handle. As I did so another one grabbed me and hand-cuffed me. Only when we reached the station did they let me see the bank deposit envelope. On it was written: 'Give me all your money or I'll smash in the screen!'

Rude corpse

Dead man's final insult

While on a peacekeeping mission in Kosovo, I found myself leading an army patrol in the capital, Pristina. As soon as we arrived, my team of three was called to a block of flats where an Albanian had shot his Serb neighbour. On arrival we found that the victim lived on the 12th floor and weighed at least 20 stone, which posed the real problem of getting the bull-sized corpse outside. I got on the radio and asked if we could throw the whale out of the window, and received a prompt ear bashing, so we lugged him out to the knackered lift. Unfortunately, after dragging him in, neither of us could reach the buttons, and it was then that I was struck by true genius. The body was in the later stages

FHM

of rigor mortis and, with Herculean strength, I managed to snap his middle finger up into a 'pointy' position and got him to press the ground floor button. He was taken to hospital 'flicking the bird,' and months later a medical friend told me of a mysterious case that his team had to deal with. They dubbed it 'The phenomenon of the pointy finger.'

Service suspended

Worker offends congregation

One Sunday morning about ten years ago, I went with my road-gang to resurface a road in Seaford. We turned up early, hoping to beat the traffic, but were somewhat dismayed to find a large number of cars parked exactly where we needed to work. There was a large church nearby, and as I was the new boy, I was sent along to see if any of the worshippers owned any of the vehicles. Inside, the vicar was right in the middle of his sermon, so I stood at the back to try to catch his eye. Just as everyone knelt down to pray, my two-way radio burst into life: 'Holy shit! What the hell are all those cars doing here?' hollered one hairy-arsed pal. 'I bet it's those bastards in the church!'

came the grumpy reply. As one, the angry congregation spun round to see a red-faced lad staggering out of church, fumbling with a radio. Needless to say we waited for the service to end before we started resurfacing the road.

Rural rage

Farmer ruins sad day

I'm a farmer in a quiet, scenic part of South Yorkshire. There are rolling fields surrounded by lakes and woods – it really is a beautiful part of the world. However, as the school summer holidays coincide with harvest-time, we do have a problem with kids. They seem to delight in setting fire to 6ft-round bales of straw and rolling them downhill, so when I spotted a group of people gathered in a field I had baled earlier I was pretty angry and tore towards them on my tractor. The sight of a ten-tonne machine hurtling across a field must be pretty frightening, and it's usually enough to send the little terrors scarpering off. But as I got nearer they refused to budge. I blared my horn and

shouted at them to get the hell out of my field. By the time I was right upon them I was furious. It was only then that I realized they were all in their forties and fifties and all wearing suits. Then an elderly lady said: 'I'm sorry, we're observing a minute's silence. We've just scattered my husband's ashes here as he loved this place so much.'

Kitchen cock-up

Diner gets unsavoury sarnie

While working as a kitchen assistant in a bistro in Australia I formed a mischievous friendship with the chef. He and I were working one New Year's Day, when the bistro took record business. In the midst of a particularly panicky period, I was trying to set up an 'avocado cheese melt' open sandwich. I laid out two slices of bread and sliced the avocado at blur speed. But in my haste, I cut myself from thumb to wrist, splattering blood all over the meal. In shock, I ran off to put a plaster on. When I came back, the sandwich had disappeared, so I just got on with the next order. Later on, when we finally had a quiet spell, I commented how quickly the chef had finished making

FHM

up the meal. He confessed: he'd just turned the avocado over and melted the cheese on top. Hey presto! Avocado cheese melt. Morbid laughter filled the kitchen area. We went to the dining area and identified the unsuspecting 'vampire', a beautiful blonde lady. Strange morbid laughter once more. A waitress came to inquire what the joke was. We recounted the tale, still hysterical. She replied, rather sternly, 'That's my best friend.' Ouch. Incidentally, the unsuspecting vampire left a big tip.

Dreadful career move

The man who dug trenches

When I was a student I was employed by a building firm during a summer holiday. Day one, start 7.30am. I was given a pick and shovel and instructed to dig a trench 40 yards long, by two feet wide and three feet deep. This took throe days. On the fourth day a surveyor came along and told the forcman that the trench was in the wrong place. I was then told to fill it in and re-dig it ten yards to the left. Four days later, tired, blistered and pissed off, I completed trench two only for another surveyor to come by and say that the first trench was correct after all and that I should fill the second trench in and re-dig the first one. I was not amused to say the least. Four days later both surveyors arrived and concluded that we didn't need any trenches and that I could just fill it in. And if they needed any more trenches dug they promised not to ask me. To this day I have a great aversion to holes.

Tank repulsion

Soldiers drink dirty water

While on exercise in Canada recently the temperature inside our armoured tank used to regularly creep above 100°F. As a consequence of this myself and my crew's intake of water was very high, even though it was usually warm enough to brew up with. During one part of the exercise while filling the internal drinking container from a jerry-can, I noticed a bad smell, which I put down to the heat of the plastic container. At dawn the following day, at the end of a particularly hot exercise, where we had to drink copious amounts of water, I decided we should all wash and clean up. I went first and very refreshing it was to wash and brush my teeth after a hard night of manoeuvres. It was then Ian, my gunner's, turn. He appeared to be having difficulty getting the remaining water from the jerry-can into the washing-up bowl. Then, with a very distinctive plop a pasty, white, hairless and obviously somewhat decayed corpse of a large rat dropped out. After a bout of dry heaving and the appropriate medical checks we then all had to endure weeks of witless Roland Rat jokes for the rest of our posting.

Salesman scammed

Oldsters terrified by desperate man

Three years ago I was constructing a house for an old couple, who lived next door. One day we were laying bricks when a sales rep called Clive arrived, asking us where the toilet was. Quick as a flash, one of the lads explained that we all used the toilet next door, and Clive immediately scuttled off towards the house. To make matters worse, the labourer told him to put the kettle on, 'And don't worry about the old lady, she's just a cleaner.'

He was gone half an hour, and when he came out he was not a happy bunny. Apparently he had put the kettle on and then wandered down the hall to find the toilet. When the old dear came out, he said, 'Hello love,

FHM

I'm just going to use the loo,' and the husband appeared and shouted, 'What the bloody hell is going on?' It was at that point Clive realized he had been stitched up, but he opted to blag it, and explained that he was a surveyor, checking for woodworm. Then he shut the toilet door and had a poo. When he emerged, the old man was standing there with a ladder and torch. 'Shall we start upstairs?' he asked, and Clive spent the next half an hour lifting up carpets checking for rotting wood.

Randy fauna

Reindeer destroys show

After graduating from college, I spent the summer working in the souvenir shop at my local zoo. At the end of October however I still didn't have a full time job lined up. With the dole queue looking inevitable, I was then fortunately approached by the marketing manager who offered me a job until January – working in Santa's grotto. In an attempt to bolster sales figures they had hit upon the idea of including a live reindeer, and being of a jovial and jolly disposition, I was told I would play the bearded gent. Before the grotto opened we had a press call, and I was chauffeur-driven up to the zoo to pose for the local journalists. Despite the enthusiastic reception from the crowd however, Prince the Reindeer was a very reluctant partner and refused to sprint alongside me for the action shots. Every time I began to run, Prince would pull in the opposite direction and knock me off my feet with a quick jerk of his head. The press persuaded me to have one last attempt, and as I pulled his reins, the mighty beast began to follow. As I turned my back to him and shouted 'Ho, ho, ho,' I suddenly felt a hoof on each shoulder. In full view of the cameras and excited children, Prince then tried to shag me. I lost my Santa beard, hat and dignity as I wrestled with the randy mass of antlers, completely unaided by his keeper who was helplessly paralysed with laughter.

Embarrassing thespian error

The actor who forgot his lines

My friend was playing the character Christopher Wren in The Mousetrap. One Friday night performance the curtain went up and the play started its seemingly perpetual motion of some 34 years. After several unremarkable entrances and bits of routine dialogue – he'd been doing eight shows a week for six months he came to his favourite scene, the part where he got to sit down on the settee and listen to the rest of the cast discuss the murderous events of the day. Musing on his strenuous partying that week while waiting for his cue he was overcome with a sense of panic at no longer recognizing the lines. Hearing someone going: 'Pssst, pssst', he looked up to the wings where he could see the Stage Manager waving him over. Uncertain whether to move for fear of missing his cue he hung on, only for the dialogue to become even more perplexing. Eventually the Stage Manager's emphatic beckoning and the small crowd of backstage staff gathered round her also signalling time-out convinced him it was time to leave the stage. When she finally hooked him into the wings she told him he'd been asleep for five minutes with the show going on around him, and to compound the felony he should have been in another part of the house providing other cast members with an alibi.

Impromptu karaoke

Solitude shattered

Two years ago, desperately short of cash, I grudgingly took a job manning the till at a petrol station. Being the new boy, I was immediately assigned the graveyard shift: 11pm to 1am, and apart from the occasional car thief and insomniac the only real company I had was my Walkman. So imagine my delight when half-way through a particularly slow, soul-destroying shift I spotted my first customer in hours, steaming past the pumps towards my booth, perhaps for an urgent pint of semi-skimmed or packet of condoms. However, as the guy got nearer it became obvious that he was not a happy bunny. It turned out that he hadn't appreciated the last 45 minutes of my

out-of-tune singalong to Semisonic over the forecourt tannoy, which I'd stupidly left switched on. Neither, it became apparent, were the rest of the nearby estate, nor my new boss, who after receiving umpteen complaints from weary locals gave me the boot.

Army high jinx

Dumped right in it

While serving in Tidworth, I heard I was being posted at short notice. As a joke, the bloke across the corridor stole my cold-weather gear and pissed all over the contents of my bergen. I only discovered this when 3,500 miles away, freezing my bollocks off and stinking of piss. Back in Blighty, I went straight out on the piss then returned to the barracks, and noticed that my practical joker pal had left his window open. I climbed in and got busy writing 'WANKER!' in toothpaste on his duvet and pissing in his coffee mug, then throwing the contents onto his posters and family photos. Finally I curled the best après-vindaloo turd you ever saw under his bed. The next morning, I was halfway through shaving when the washroom door burst open and a 6ft 7in, 18-stone former Hampshire Schoolboys' lock-forward burst in and barked, 'Who's the fuckin' dead man who's shit under my bed and thrown piss at my parents?' I could barely hold my razor still. My previous neighbour had been posted to a new regiment while I was away. Please don't reveal my name – big, bad Gaz is still on the look-out.

Strange religious vision

Driver leaves moving car

A few years ago I worked in an estate agent's office on the corner of a busy high road at the top of a gentle hill. We all parked our company cars on the side street. One Monday morning my car was parked close to the junction, in full view of the office. Someone noticed an old green Fiesta trundling around the corner, with three elderly ladies as passengers, no driver, the driver's door open and another elderly lady, dressed in black, running behind the car, shouting. She caught up with it just as it crashed into the back of my parked company car. My colleagues and I rushed out with me screaming for an explanation. The elderly lady turned on me, shocked at my bad language, and I saw

FHM

that the black outfit was actually that of a nun. Her passenger, the Mother Superior, explained that Sister Mary had offered to nip into Boots on the opposite corner, but had forgotten she was driving and just stepped out of the slightly moving car, quickly realizing her mistake. With a wry smile my boss said to the Mother Superior: 'You realize the insurance will never pay up?' 'Why?' asked the horrified nun. 'Act of God,' he mused. The insurance did pay.

Candid camera

Gaseous escape captured

When I worked for a defence company, I was involved in a missile test. This sounds exciting, but in reality it meant spending a couple of weeks sitting in a concrete bunker waiting for the day to end, and the evening drinking to start. Early one morning, after a particularly heavy night on the ale, I was stuck as normal in my concrete prison – with no chance to get rid of the foul gas my digestive system was producing from the night before. So when someone asked me to go outside to adjust some equipment, I jumped at the chance, and within minutes had let rip with a by now considerable beer fart. After a few minutes spent freezing my arse off, I returned to the bunker, to find

everyone gathered around a monitor, killing themselves laughing. I wandered over to take a look and watched as the clearly discernible infrared image of a person came into view, stopped, and bent over. The thermal display from my fart was actually quite impressive, and some clever sod even made it into a screensaver as my leaving present.

Chompers hidden

Pensioner loses teeth

One of the few highlights of working on an acute medical ward centred around a sweet old dear who was admitted with severe dementia. It quickly became apparent that she was constipated and would need suppositories to get things going, which she claimed she could do herself. Later that morning, while she was getting washed, an enquiry was made on the whereabouts of her false teeth, to which she replied that she had stuck them up her arse. Finding the suppositories floating in her cornflakes, we decided that she could be right, and whisked her off to X-ray. Sadly, nothing was found. A week later she was still bunged up, so I gave her a mild enema and told her

I'd be back in a few minutes. When I returned I was greeted by the sight of granny bending over the bed, with her winking starfish aimed squarely at my face. Then, as I rushed to help her, her arse slowly changed shape, and three front teeth briefly surfaced before being sucked back in. I stood there as her bottom grinned, then frowned at me, until the top set of chompers finally came flying out, followed by a wave of shit. To this day, the bottom set are still missing.

Princess nightmare

Royal nearly gassed on plane

While working as a crew member for an airline, we had to do a short hop from the Bahamas to Trinidad and back. After the passengers had boarded, news soon filtered down to 'chaos class' that Princess Anne and her entourage would be getting on, and that first class was a no-go area for us plebs working in economy. Unfortunately, I had unwisely tried a few of the local 'delicacies' and was subsequently suffering from a bad case of the trots, and the accompanying symptom known locally as 'Caribbean Ring'. Soon after take-off, my bowels decided to evacuate. I couldn't find a free toilet anywhere in the non-cordoned-off area of the plane, so I trespassed into a

FHM

first class loo, where I unloaded the foulest toxic waste ever known outside Chernobyl. With my business done, I opened the door only to find myself face to face with HRH. After nervously bowing, I sped away, pausing only to glance back and watched her enter that gas chamber. At the very least, I hope I left the seat warm.

Decorating disaster

Painter flees embarrassment

When I was struggling to earn a crust, and willing to take any work for any price, I once landed a job painting a friend of a friend's parents' house. I went round there on my first day and talked over the colours and details with the owners, then they left me to get on with it. I moved all of the furniture in their living room into the centre of the room, including the big old piano, which I then covered in dust sheets. All seemed to be going well. I did the walls, then began on the woodwork with a lovely deep blue gloss the owners had chosen. Painting the picture rail, I rested the tin of gloss on the piano. After I had finished the first coat, I went to move the tin and noticed with

FHM

horror that a huge pool of blue paint had leaked through a hole in the dust sheet, and was already half set on the instrument's French-polished surface. I panicked. Instead of carefully trying to clean up my mess, I rubbed it off with sandpaper, ruining the surface forever. I then packed up my things and left, with the room half-painted, the piano a wreck, and a friend of a friend having to be avoided for the rest of my life.

Hotel Horrors

Tourist fouls up relationship

On the first night my girlfriend and I spent in our hotel in the USA, I blocked the toilet and coated the bathroom floor in poo. Later that week, after a heavy seafood and beer session, I started suffering a growling gut that must have woken the place. Giving in to the call of the toilet, I dropped my kecks seconds before the world fell out of my arse. I exited the bathroom swiftly, to avoid being caught by the probable overflow that would follow such a marathon session on the shitter. As I dived into bed, I noticed that it was all hot and sticky: my arse had leaked all of its vile contents during my drunken slumber! I grabbed a nearby bog roll, trying to mop it up. But I'd wrought

FHM

such anal devastation that my girlfriend's leg was smeared in shit, and she was half-lying in a pool of foul-smelling liquid. When a length of bog roll stuck to her leg and would not come off, I returned, defeated, to the bog, upon which I fell asleep. I awoke to a knock on the bathroom door, and my shit-smeared girlfriend, looking terribly embarrassed, said, 'I'm really sorry, I think I had an accident.' My male survival instincts kicked in, and I slyly countered, 'I know, that's why I had to sleep in here all night.' To this day, although I remain justly proud of the event, I cannot bring myself to tell her the truth.

Cruiser slips

Drunken jig ends in disaster

A few years ago during a holiday in Mallorca, myself and six mates went on a booze cruise. After downing gallons of ale as our small vessel pootled round the bay, the boat anchored and my mates proceeded to dance on the deck. However, seeing their antics, the organizer warned everyone to be careful as it was very slippery. My mates duly stopped and sloped off for a swim, leaving me to finish my drink in peace. Soon I decided to join them and walked round the boat towards the steps which led into the sea, only to encounter a buxom lassie coming the other way. As we attempted to pass each other, I decided to make a joke of the situation and, grinning, began dancing like a constipated elephant. Of course, I immediately lost my footing and, as my feet went from beneath me, they connected with the girl's legs, drop-kicking her straight over the side and into the sea. We stuck to dry land from that day on.

Disaster at 20,000ft

Tourist in toilet trauma

Last Christmas I was on a overnight flight to the Gambia with my girlfriend and her parents who had kindly bought us a two-week break as a present. I was sitting in the aisle seat, with my prospective father-in-law opposite me. To break the ice, we shared a drink or two and it wasn't long before the large quantity I was consuming at altitude made me feel rather light-headed. As the lights in the cabin began to extinguish, there was no option but to adjourn to the little boys' room to relieve my bladder. I had mistimed badly and was leaking slightly as I tried to open the small door. I already had my flies undone and my old fella at the ready. As soon as I swung the door open, I rushed in, closed my eyes and enjoyed the immense pleasure that only such relief can bring. It then came to my attention that, instead of the delightful tinkling noise that I was expecting, there was more of a bass-like thud. It was too dark to see what was happening, so I finished what I had started and returned to my seat. When I next woke up I was dismayed to learn that there was to be no in-flight meal as the trolley which was kept in a room at the back had suffered a mishap.

Hot shot

Lovers face wrath of insomniac

My holiday in Mexico was going splendidly until an obnoxious American couple moved in next door. Every night they would keep us awake with their sexual marathons; loud slapping noises interjected with the occasional scream, groan and, on one occasion, the encouraging voices of another couple. Despite my complaints to the manager, the noise continued, so I decided to take matters into my own hands. Early one morning I got the wife to engage them in conversation while I dived over the balcony and doused the loud lady's bikini gusset with Mexican white pepper. Then we went to the swimming pool to await the results. Sadly, despite watching them swim for over an hour, nothing happened, and we retreated utterly defeated for another sleepless night. In the early hours of the morning, however, we suddenly heard a Yank voice announce: 'Gee honey, my cock is on fucking fire,' followed by an ear-piercing scream from his wife. Our only conclusion was that the pepper had somehow got inside her, and only made itself known once they had started shagging. We didn't get a peep out of them for the remaining four days.

Bottle-smashing furore

Tourists wind up french

I was staying on a French campsite with two friends. On our last night we got friendly with a couple of French girls and Dave, who spoke the language fluently. We all got very drunk and, at 5am, there were a million broken beer bottles strewn across the campsite car park, but we just went to the beach to sleep it off. On our return to the scene we were greeted by a trio of irate Frenchmen – the owner of the campsite, the proprietor of a hotel whose guests had been kept awake all night, and a motorcycle cop. It was clear these Gauls were after our balls. Things were looking very merde-like when all of a sudden the cavalry arrived. Dave. He asked what the problem was and went off on the most passionate speech about … what? We were clueless. When Dave stopped for breath, the Frenchmen looked at us with a sort of nostalgic fondness, smiled weakly, shook each of our hands and left. Apparently, we were grandsons of English war heroes who perished in the D-Day landings, here to celebrate the memories of our relatives in true English fashion – by raising a glass or a thousand, then smashing them all.

Nude photo shame

Tourist's vacation mishap

While travelling around Europe a few years ago, I ended up on the Greek island of Ios. Now Ios has the reputation of being a wild and outrageous resort, so after pitching our tent at the nearest campsite, my mate and I set off to explore. We trawled the bars and clubs and got absolutely leathered. The next morning I was woken by the distant giggle of women and the whirr of camera shutters. As I slowly came to, I realized I was lying on my back in the blazing sun. I tried opening my eyes, squinting at the blinding light, and lifting my medicine ball head to survey my surroundings. After a few minutes it all started coming back to me. I had indeed made it back to the campsite, but hadn't managed to get inside the tent, so after peeling off completely, I'd slept where I'd fallen. To my horror, I found that I'd been sleeping on my back, all morning, in front of the main entrance to the camp, bollock naked and with a hard-on like a blind cobbler's thumb.

I've often wondered how many photo albums across the world my morning glory now adorns.

Nautical hygiene worry

Makeshift tea urn scenario

Early morning on a cold Saturday about ten years ago, four artists, a printer, a photographer, an account executive and myself sailed five miles out from the Essex coast on a day's mission to catch a whopper. About 6.30 am I went in search of the loo, to be told in a roundabout way that all bodily functions were to be released over the side. At about eight, the skipper came topside with a fag in his mouth and a plastic washing-up bowl in his hands, containing eight cups of a piping hot drink and a plate full of sandwiches. Once finished, he collected the mugs and returned below deck. Within a couple of minutes he was back, yet again clutching the plastic bowl. He moved to the front of the boat and threw the contents of the bowl over the side. Seconds later a huge turd floated past our side of the boat. Bob, David and myself looked at each other in disbelief and burst out laughing. The thing was absolutely huge. Only the three of us had seen what had gone on, and within seconds of going down below the skipper emerged once again from his hole clutching the bowl with yet more food and drinks in it. The three on our side of the boat gave his menu a wide berth for the rest of the trip, while the five on the port side imagined they were getting preferential treatment.

Amsterdam shocker

Drunk man shamed

Last year a group of us went to Amsterdam for the
weekend for a beery break. On the first night we did
the usual: got hammered and had a good look at the
huge variety of strippers on show. Out of the six of us
that were there one of my mates decided he was
having too much of a laugh in the transvestite bar, and
refused to come back to the hotel with the rest of us.
At about five o'clock in the morning we heard him
stagger into the hotel, causing a commotion as he
banged his way along the corridor. By the time he got
to our room we were all awake. He was completely
bladdered and could not even talk. Within seconds of
hitting the bed he was fast asleep, and it was then

that the rest of us decided to wind him up. I spat into a condom, pulled down his pants, and poked the condom up his arse with a pen. Then we pulled his pants back up and left him to sleep. The next morning at breakfast we asked him how he had got on after we'd left, but he refused to talk. He stayed in his room for the whole day, claiming he was too hung-over to come out. That evening he also refused to join us. On the last day of our holiday we finally asked him if he had taken the condom out of his arse. He lost it. He dived across the table and punched me in the face. It took ages before he eventually saw the funny side.

Seaside horror

Men sleep on dead mammal

Several years ago, a group of friends and I set off on our motorbikes for a day in Great Yarmouth. After an uneventful trip, we hit the local hostelries, and six hours later decided to find a place to stay for the night. Unfortunately, as it was high season, most accommodation was fully booked and those places that weren't were unwilling to put up a dozen pissed bikers. Finally, most of us found places to stay, but two mates who were more pissed than the rest of us said they were going to crash out on the local beach. We arranged to meet up in the car park of a café at 9.30 am the next morning.

When we all met up as planned, the two lads who

had slept on the beach turned up looking a bit sorry for themselves and stinking like a sewage farm. When asked what had happened, they told us that they had crashed on the beach at high tide, where they had found what they thought was a mound of tarpaulin. But when they woke that morning, they were horrified to discover that what had been keeping them warm all night was, in fact, the bloated carcass of a not-so-recently-deceased seal.

Camp thugs

Squealer dumped by gang

Back in the summer of 1992, I was participating in a Duke of Edinburgh Silver Award camping trip with several of my school friends. The trip was scheduled to last for three days, and on the first night a group of us decided to go to the village shop to get some beer. The night went well until one lad, who hadn't been invited to our shindig, blabbed to the teachers. We promptly got a bollocking and were threatened with expulsion if we did it again. Later that same night, when the grass was asleep in his bag, we tied belts around his arms and legs and gagged him with an old sock. We then carried him over a couple of fields and dropped him in one of those old wooden cow troughs.

The water didn't cover him, so he lay in the few inches of mess at the bottom. We then went back to our tents, planning to pick the mug up a few hours later. At 6am the next morning we were woken by our furious group leaders: the human slug had crawled across the fields inside his bag and turned up at camp. We were excluded from the award and made to buy the bastard a new bag.

Dental disaster

Laughing turk extracts tooth

Last year I went on holiday to Mersin in Turkey. Basically, the break was to be an eating and drinking extravaganza. The days blurred into one another and everything was going well on what was turning out to be the holiday of a lifetime, until disaster – I woke up one morning with a toothache which simply wouldn't go away. The agony proved so great that I had to go down to the hotel reception and explain to the bilingual girl behind the counter that I thought I was dying. She very kindly took me to a dental clinic: no moody affair with a rickety chair and a pair of pliers, but a professional-looking place. Anyway, the girl explained my dilemma. The dentist put me in the chair and looked into my mouth, then he injected my gum, making everything numb. Finally, and so quickly that I couldn't believe it had happened, he whipped my tooth out. I was stunned – and even more so when, cleaning out my mouth, he started to laugh. I asked the girl to translate for me and it turned out that, on closer examination, the dentist had realized I simply had a piece of garlic sausage stuck in my gum, and that the tooth hadn't needed to come out at all.

Country violence

Lad clumped for beer error

Last summer, a friend and I decided to go on a bike ride into the countryside around Nottingham. After several hours of hard riding, we thought we should find a nice country pub and have a few pints to cool off. We walked into a pub full of villagers and local farmers, all of whom started to stare at us as we made our way to the bar. My friend got the drinks in as I nervously looked around the pub, trying to appear relaxed. For some reason, my eyes were drawn to the Guinness pump – the one shaped like a glass of the stuff. Taking anything to be a welcome distraction from the nasty looks I was getting from the other punters, I reached over to the pump and, to my horror, saw my fingers disappear into the head of a genuine pint of Guinness. The huge farmer at the bar whose pint it was didn't even let me finish the first word of an explanation: he smashed me to the floor immediately. Both my friend and I were then physically ejected from the pub without getting a sip of drink.

Foreign fiasco

Traveller has toilet trouble

I had been cooped up with seven people on a sailing holiday around the Greek islands on a 38ft (11.5m) yacht for two weeks. After a long, hot day at sea, we entered a harbour to moor up and relax for a few days. I was feeling the urge to splurge, but discovered that nobody had emptied the bilge tank. As the toilet became unusable for the next two days, a friend and I trekked off into the town and found a bar with a toilet. By now, I was facing the biggest evacuation since *Towering Inferno*. I opened the door to find a pan in an area big enough to swing a kitten. There was no light, window or lock. I called to my mate and asked him to stand guard. By leaving the door open and keeping my foot against it to make a one-inch gap, I had just enough light to allow me to place my bare behind on the seat. But when it came time to wipe up, it wasn't possible to maintain the gap in the door without it swinging open, so I shut it. I was now in complete darkness. I fumbled around until I placed my hand on some paper – and pulled. Now, you must understand that this was my first time in Greece and I didn't realize that when disposing of used toilet paper, due to their poor sewage system, they put it into a bin. I was pulling at someone else's waste! Not unsurprisingly, the closest I ever go to Greece now is a chicken kebab on a Friday night.

Filthy tosser

Man caught out by spanish glass

Three mates and I went to Ibiza for two weeks. A few days into the holiday, three of us were sitting by the hotel pool when some girls came over and asked if we were in the flat overlooking the main road. When we said we were, they laughed and said we'd better hang a towel across the window – which went from floor to ceiling and appeared frosted from the inside – because it was totally clear from the café across the road and everybody could see us showering. Slightly embarrassed, we made our way back to the flat. Later on that evening our fourth friend, who hadn't heard about the window, went to have his shower. We thought it would be a laugh not to tell him about the 'view' and went across to the café, pointing out the spectacle to fellow holiday-makers. Imagine our horror as our mate started to have a wank. Worse still, he put the shower head to unusual and good effect. After all manner of contortions I thought enough was enough, and knocked on the bathroom door and told him to stick his head out of the window. When he did he was greeted with a loud cheer from the crowd below, and he spent the rest of the holiday refusing to leave the apartment.

Mistaken identity

Australian makes stars appear

Many years ago, after being bored rigid by friends'
tales of foreign adventure, my mate Nigel and I went
to Australia to see what all the fuss was about. We
ended up in Bondi, and one afternoon we were
walking home when Nigel nudged me and pointed out
the British actor Terence Stamp. I knew it was him, but
for no real reason, I said he looked nothing like Mr
Stamp, and teased him all the way home, pointing at
people with moustaches and shouting, 'Look, Burt
Reynolds!' He finally snapped, and marched back to
find our great actor. We found him sitting in the
window of a local café, minding his own business with
a coffee and paper. 'See, it is him,' said Nigel

triumphantly, but I just laughed and said Terence had bigger ears. Terence couldn't help but notice two men pointing at him through the glass, and he started to look rather irate. Nigel then started stopping people in the street to get their opinion, even going so far as to knock loudly on the glass, until Stamp could take no more. He sprinted out the door, and it wasn't until he was within a yard of us that we realized two things: he wanted a fight, and it wasn't Terence Stamp. Suffice to say, Nigel had the shit kicked out of him by Australia's best look-alike.

Ski accident

Holiday-maker cut short

A few years ago I went on a skiing holiday with friends to a resort in Switzerland. On the first day we caught the cable car, and at the top of the mountain one of the girls in our group decided that she needed to pee. The only available loo was in a terrible condition however, and she convinced herself that she could hold on until she reached the bottom of the slopes. About 300 yards down the hill she realized that she had been wrong, and we waited for her as she promptly skied off into the woods that ran down the left side of the run. Trying to be as quick as possible, she decided against removing her skis, opting instead to simply drop her salopettes, crouch down, and hold

FHM

onto an overhanging branch. We then heard a loud snap as the branch broke, and could only watch in awe as she came bombing out of the shrubbery, naked from the waist down with her trousers around her ankles, and clutching the remnants of a branch. The lift station was about 50 yards below her, and she crashed into about 500 people standing patiently in the queue. Although they all saw the funny side, she spent the rest of the holiday hiding in the hotel.

Dirty-talk disaster

Sexual ignorance exposed

I was out with my mates in the local nightclub, when a horny babe came up to me on the dancefloor and started talking really dirty. Astounded by my good fortune, I left my pint and my mates and disappeared outside with her. While searching for a suitable spot to do the dirty deed, I came across a secluded path surrounded by bushes. Perfect. Within seconds we were in the throes of passion, she whispered, 'Put me on the cross, put me on the cross.' Thinking she was moaning to herself, I carried on, but moments later she moaned again, 'Put me on the cross.' Baffled by her rambling, I still carried on regardless. Minutes later, she moaned even louder, 'Put me on the cross.'

By now I was beginning to think she knew some sexual position I didn't. Not wanting to appear incompetent, I grabbed her arms, pinned them at right angles to her body, put her legs together so she was in the shape of a crucifix, and kept on pumping. 'What the hell are you doing?' she cried. 'Putting you on the cross,' I said confidently. She replied, 'I said to put me on the grass, these bloody stones are hurting my back.'

Live sex in soho

Exhibitionists in the dark

I had been pursuing a dark beauty from Sierra Leone for several months. Her defences eventually came down and we became a couple. I decided, one weekend, to treat her to a West End show and then a meal in Soho. In the restaurant, we got closer and closer, touching parts of each other that shouldn't really be touched in public … So, we paid the bill and escaped quickly, scrabbling over the fence into the garden in the middle of Soho Square for a bit of privacy. On a patch of grass, we started to kiss and grope each other. Before we knew it, we were buck naked and humping away. We were loving every minute of it, but, unfortunately our attention was focused on each other and not on the crowd of men from a nearby gay bar who had gathered to watch. Once we realized what was going on, my girlfriend and I really got off on all the attention we were getting. However, we didn't realize that, due to my girlfriend's colour, our audience couldn't see her in the dark. Only my big white butt was visible, as it furiously moved up and down on the grass. Presumably, the various characters from the bar thought I was having sex with a hole in the ground.

Seaside shag

Couple have filthy sex

It was to be a romantic weekend away for myself, my girlfriend and another couple. We drove up to Hunstanton on a hot summer's day, parked the car and set off along the beach with our provisions: plenty of drink and some food for cooking on the driftwood fires we planned to build. We set up camp, sipped red wine and ate sausages cooked in cider as the sun went down. The tide drifted out, and the moon rose as the fire slowly died. My mate and his girl went for a walk, while I decided to hit the hay with my new love. We walked back up the beach to a row of beach huts, giggling all the while, and broke into one. We drunkenly fell to the floor and had a great sweaty sex session, before falling into deep slumber. In the morning I woke up and curiously patted the crunchy floor of the cabin with my hands. My girlfriend did the same. As my mate swung the door open and sunlight bathed the room, we were all disgusted to see that we had spent our night of passion on a carpet made up of millions of dead flies.

Caught in the act

The dog gets it

One summer I was at a mate's house revising for impending exams. Having spent several hours studying intensively, we were both in need of a break. My mate suggested we reward our hard work by watching one of his brother's porno videos. Within minutes of watching an on-screen orgy, my teenage libido was in overdrive and I needed a wank. Casting an eye across the room, I could see my mate was thinking the same. Not wanting to miss any action, I simply put my hand down the front of my trousers. After ten minutes, my attention was drawn to movement out of the corner of my eye. To my utter horror, my mate's mum had returned home early and was making her way towards the back door. I froze as she looked in through the patio doors, pointing at us with her mouth wide open. 'How many times have I warned you about this,' she bellowed as she entered the lounge. 'I've told you time and time again, you'll get hairs all over the furniture!' I was about to make my excuses when she interrupted. 'Don't let Sandy on the furniture!' she bellowed. Then, with immense relief, the penny dropped. Somehow she had looked straight past the two of us abusing ourselves and had spotted Sandy, the border collie, sitting on a chair at the far end of the room.

Washing machine woe

Kitchen sex curtailed

I was once seeing a girl who was renting a room in a house where the washing machine was always breaking down. Whenever her housemate was out, we grabbed the opportunity to make love, and often didn't even make it to the bedroom in our passion. One morning, my girlfriend had agreed to stay in as a man was coming round to fix the washing machine once and for all; we had waited days for an appointment and of course, he hadn't turned up the first time he promised to. We were in the kitchen when we started kissing. After about 30 seconds we were both minus our clothes and using the worktop for our enjoyment. This became a screaming session and most of the screaming came from me. In the (occasional) quiet moments, I could dimly hear voices – I thought it was the TV – and suddenly I saw someone walking through the lounge towards the kitchen. We froze for a moment, then both grabbed what we could and tried to get dressed. But it was going to be too late. Panicking, I walked into the lounge, stark bollock naked, holding a pile of clothes and shouted back into the kitchen without thinking, 'Darling, can you get the rest of the clothes out of the washing machine, they're done.' The plumber looked me up and down in a bemused way and said, 'Has it been fixed? I'll be going then.'

Whore's bath

Costly wipe-down

A few years ago I made it my aim in life to pull the gorgeous Irish barmaid in my local, and after several weeks' flirting I finally asked her out. Not only did she say yes, but the rest of the night went so well that she invited me back to her house. After snogging in the taxi, we arrived at hers. As she went to the toilet I was left in a bit of a panic: I hadn't showered that morning. As things were going so well it seemed only a matter of minutes before my old fella would be brought into action, so I crept into the darkened kitchen and gave myself a bit of a clean 'south of the border' with a handy flannel. She soon returned and, sure enough, we got straight down to it, with me lying on the couch

FHM

while she went down on me. But no sooner had her lips touched my bits than she straightened up. 'What's that?' she asked, pointing to my pubes. On inspection I saw a solitary baked bean nestled among the curly hairs – the 'flannel' I'd used had, in fact, been a dirty dishcloth. I left red-faced and never saw her again.

Unwelcome surprise

Birthday boy gets caught out

My friend, an airman, had his 21st birthday a few weeks before being posted to Saudi Arabia. His parents asked if he would like a big party to celebrate. He declined the offer, asking instead if he could have a quiet evening at home with his girlfriend, cook her a meal, candles, soft music – and, while his parents were out, a good sex session to keep him going for the four months he'd be away. So, the night came, his parents went out, and a fine meal was prepared. The wine flowed and eventually the pair were rolling around the living room in their favourite position: the 69. While in full swing the phone rang. 'Let's answer it in this position,' my friend suggested, and off they wriggled into the hall. It was his mother on her mobile. 'Your dad thinks he's left his glasses in the kitchen, can you check, please,' she said. Once again, he suggested they stay in the position. 'It'll be a laugh,' he said. Off they wriggled again, laughing all the way. 'Surprise, surprise! Happy birthday!' was their greeting as they opened the door. And, of course, Mum, Dad, Grandma, aunties, uncles and cousins were all there to congratulate the young man, bless them.

Radio exposure

Student DJ goes bonkers for bingo

While at university a few years ago, I was fortunate enough to land a slot on the campus radio. It was a position I turned to my advantage to cultivate an image of hip and coolness – which surprisingly pulled the girls. I would often taken my conquests back to the studio, which I used as a secret shag pad. One evening, I took a girl back there and we started messing about with a bingo game which the station used. We called out the numbers and took our clothes off as a forfeit. Eventually we were both butt-naked as I pulled out a final fake forfeit, which said 'Spread your legs and think of England.' There then ensued a frantic bout of shagging, culminating in the girl shouting,

'House! Bingo!' while in the throes of ecstasy. The following day, we were mortified when walking around campus as fellow students pointed and nudged, with cries of 'Bingo!' It seems I'd inadvertently knocked the broadcast switch on during our high jinks and some community-spirited listener had informed as many people as he could.

Office sex

Coffee cream

Recently I decided to start seeing a work colleague. Bearing in mind that I work in an office with over 20 females and only two males, my years of office celibacy were highly commendable – or stupid! So one Sunday, said colleague and I were working hard, when she challenged me to a bout of shagging round the office! Always up for a challenge, I duly obliged. After 45 minutes' worth of some of the best nookie I've ever had, it was time to cover our tracks. We had, however, left a 'wet patch' on one desk and, agonizingly, there was not a jot of toilet paper in the whole damn office. Using our initiative, we grabbed a tea towel, wiped up and made tracks home! Imagine my horror the next

day when, with clients arriving at 9.15am, a secretary was wiping the cups with the same towel we'd used not 12 hours earlier. My guilt was further increased when the client noted a peculiar taste on the rim of his cup! The towel, which had an oddly musky smell, was identified as the culprit. No-one could identify this odour; the offending item was sent for a wash and the client given a clean cup.

Bathroom shocker

Shag brings out firemen

When I was a student I lived in a 'mixed' household, which thankfully meant that the boys and the girls all lived together. My girlfriend at the time was a lively lass, and liked to experiment sexually. With this in mind she arranged for us to have a sexy bath together one evening when all the other students were out 'studying'. We lit the draughty old bathroom with candles which we rested on the window sill, filled the bath to the brim with bubbles, and slipped into the water for some serious cleansing. Suddenly, just as I was soaping some interesting body parts, and having some of mine vigorously rubbed clean, there was a thundering crash at the door, followed by loud shouting. Two security guards were battering down the door with fire extinguishers. After a few seconds of stunned silence from both sides they started to piss themselves with laughter. It seems they had been patrolling the grounds near our house and had seen a 'massive fire' in one of our windows. Our flickering candles, through the frosted glass, had led them to storm in on our sexy bubble-bath. After they had left we couldn't quite recreate the atmosphere, so the whole night was a write-off.

Trainee fireman

Passion causes inferno

A few years ago I was seeing a young girl who still lived with her parents. Every Thursday evening I would go round to her house and disappear upstairs with her to 'play on her PC'. This particular evening she had some perfumed candles littered around the place, and we got straight down to things. I kept the groans to a minimum so that her parents wouldn't become suspicious, and after we had finished I slipped off the condom, dropped it in the bin, and snuggled back up with my girl. It was then that I noticed the smell of burning and realized that one of the candles had set fire to the bin's contents – basically a load of tissues and a used rubber johnny. As I leapt out of bed, I accidentally kicked the contents across the room, and we suddenly had a serious fire on our hands. So naked as the day I was born, I heroically grabbed the nearest thing – a 10-inch (25-cm) rubber dildo that we used for foreplay – and began beating the carpet furiously. And then her father burst through the door shouting, 'What's all the noise about up here?' Needless to say, I took advantage of his few moments of shocked disbelief, grabbed my trousers and legged it, pausing only once to throw a blackened plastic cock into their hedge.

Mistake with pants

Bragging leads to red face

After a busy evening clubbing, I found myself being taken home by a young divorcee for a night of passion. We paid off her baby-sitter and settled down to the evening's entertainment. Having to work the next day – and wanting to escape – I awoke early and left my conquest asleep. I noticed a pair of ski pants lying in a tangled mess with a pair of knickers inside them. I immediately retrieved the underwear as a trophy and stuffed them in my trouser pocket. I went straight to work and during my mid-morning tea break, I entertained my colleagues with tales of my previous night's exploits. I spared no detail and played to the crowd, building up to the finale: the unveiling of my lady friend's underwear. At the appropriate point, I whipped out the aforementioned smalls and proudly held them aloft. It was only when I saw my workmate's shocked faces that I lowered my arms to find not the scanty women's knickers I was expecting, but a tiny pair of slightly soiled cotton briefs. Last owner: my sexual partner's four-year-old daughter!

Disastrous leak

Novelty balloon

Believe me, safe sex can get messy. On the final leg of an infamous pub crawl I spotted a gorgeous redhead. Egged on by my mates, I decided to go over and chat her up. We got on great and the conversation and drinks flowed until closing time. By the time we left the pub, we couldn't keep our hands off each other. However, as Debbie lived with her parents and I lived with mine, we decided there was only one thing for it – we would have to have sex under the stars. So, I found myself on my back in a field, with Debbie riding me senseless. After the deed was done I had an urgent need to empty my, by now bursting, bladder. I staggered over to some trees and promptly began to

relieve myself. I felt the customary warm sensation but realized that I couldn't hear the familiar sound of pee. I looked down and, in the moonlight, noticed I'd forgotten to remove the condom, which by now was inflated like a balloon with my piss. Before I could react, the weight of fluid pulled the condom off my cock, drenching my trousers and shoes in the process. Debbie, who had witnessed all this, was so impressed that she left me to stagger home on my own and completely avoided me in the future.

Horror with pants

Tourist's toilet trauma

While on a business trip to France, I was invited to a party in a bar. Soon I got talking to a stunning girl, Francine. A shag seemed an absolute certainty, so I got fairly pissed. Suddenly I felt the need to have a crap, so I told Francine I'd be back. Spotting a sign saying 'Hommes', I made a mad dash and found myself in a dark alley behind the café with a door at the end. Inside was a typical French bog: two footplates and a septic hole in the ground. I dropped my kecks and laid cable, which proved to be pretty nasty. Then I realized that there was no paper. A sock just wasn't going to do the trick, so I decided to use my boxer shorts. Removing them required a real balancing act: I always had to keep one shoe on and not fall into the mire below. I couldn't leave the soiled boxers in the trap so I went out into the alley to find a bin. Just then, the far door opened, and Francine appeared. So I panicked and lobbed the boxers onto the roof of the khazi. She walked slowly towards me. I lit a cigarette. She came up, I leaned down to kiss her – and suddenly there was a rolling noise, then a splat next to my left shoe, as if a wet packet of sand had just fallen. It was my 'turd-ridden' boxers, which I had thrown onto a sloping roof. I spent the night alone.

Unprincipled seaman

Man cheats to win bike

A couple of years ago, while on home leave from the Navy in my home town of Cockermouth, I was asked to take my little brother to the local Donkey Derby. On arrival we saw helium balloons floating in the breeze, and realized there was some sort of competition going on. We wandered off to find the relevant stand, and discovered that for 50p you could buy a ticket, leave your name and address, and attach half the ticket to the balloon. After a certain amount of time the ticket which had been sent back from the most distant place from the fair won a top-of-the-range mountain bike. I duly bought a balloon, filled in my details and let it go. My brother, however, simply wanted something to play around with, so I bought another one for 50p, pocketed the ticket stub and gave him the balloon. We enjoyed the rest of the day, and I thought no more about the incident until I went back to my ship in Portsmouth. On looking in my wallet, I found I still had the ticket from my brother's balloon. Our next port of call was the Canary Islands: I duly posted back the ticket and my brother received a nice new mountain bike, all courtesy of his dishonest older brother. To make matters worse, when next back home I sold the bike and went out on the piss for a couple of days on the proceeds.

Thoughtless prank

Sprain causes night of terror

When I was at school, we used to play a game in our dinner break which involved locking some unsuspecting young lad in one of the lockers. The idea was that we'd roll the locker onto its side, kick it for a bit, then let the poor bugger out, who would usually stumble around dazed for a few minutes. One dinner break we locked someone in, rolled the locker over and gave it our customary kick, then couldn't unlock it. At first our prisoner thought we were joking, only realizing things were a little more serious when he heard the key snap in the lock. Dinner break ended and we still couldn't force open the locker, so I promised I'd return after school to let him out. But we had PE in the afternoon and I sprained my ankle playing football. Such was the pain, I caught the school bus straight home. It wasn't until later that evening that I remembered the locker, when my mum came off the phone saying, 'I've got Mrs Thompson on in a bit of a state, wondering if you've seen her boy, as he didn't come home from school.' I daren't own up at the time, but did get to school very early in the morning, only to be confronted by the police, the caretaker – with crow-bar – and the gasping boy.

Feline surprise

Cat pierces love balloon

Last Christmas Eve, after a heavy week on the beers, I found myself in the company of a very attractive girl. Somehow I managed to convince her to invite me home, and despite our drunken state we found a condom and got down to business, before eventually nodding off. Sometime later I was woken by the sound of her alarm clock, and as she made no attempt to get up and turn it off, I jumped out of bed, and staggered around in the darkness until I found it. I then felt her cat jump up between my legs, and as the girl had woken up, I asked her to turn the lamp on. Glancing down, I then noticed that the condom I had been wearing was still attached to my knob. Worse, I had inadvertently managed to piss myself during the night, and the whole bulbous mass was swaying wildly between my legs. Then, as the pair of us stared in horror, the cat made a final leap and speared the balloon with its razor-sharp talons, covering the room in cold sperm and urine. I left so quickly, I never even found out her name.

Bolshy brothers

Drawing-pin drama

When young, it was not uncommon for my brother and I to engage in a bit of sibling fighting. One particular balmy night, we were too feisty to sleep. As my parents relaxed downstairs in front of the TV, I crept from my bedroom and into my brother's, where I set about knocking eight bells out of him with a pillow. The commotion led to shouts from downstairs for us to cease our rowdy fighting and get back to bed. However, a few minutes later, I was on the receiving end of an attack. This time my father bounded in, warning us that if he heard so much as another whisper, there would be trouble. He was a man who commanded respect, and we meekly returned to our beds. But there must have been mischief in the air that night, because I soon found myself creeping into my brother's room for one last belt – but he had scattered drawing pins across the threshold to his room! As I stole into the darkness, I miraculously avoided the many tacks that lay across my path, and set about pummelling the startled youth. His cries alerted my furious parents, and as my father's footsteps pounded the stairs I scurried out the room – incredibly missing the tacks again – just in time to witness dad's bare feet sinking into the drawing pins. You can imagine the rest.

Royal shame

Child spoils the big day

It was 1981, and the country was gripped with Royal Wedding fever as Prince Charles and Lady Di got set to tie the knot. My parents, being staunch supporters of the royal family, decided to drag my younger brother and I down to Buckingham Palace so we could see the happy couple out on the balcony. Naturally, the nation's capital was heaving, and the throng around Buck House was awesome. Being an inquisitive ten-year-old, I wormed my way through the grown-ups' legs right to the very front of the crowd and stuck my head through the Palace railings – where it remained firmly wedged when I tried to pull it out. The next thing I knew I had a policeman on one leg, my dad on the other and my mum smearing margarine, kindly donated by a fat man from a hamburger stand, all over my ears. Nothing worked. Eventually a huge section of the crowd had to move out of the way so that a fire engine could get up to the fence. They had to cut a section out of the fence (which I wasn't allowed to keep as a souvenir) to free me, and the whole story made the papers. I not only ruined the day for my parents and a large section of the crowd, I was also responsible for an act of vandalism on the home of our great Queen. I apologize.

Gift delivered

Red face for souvenir hunter

During an all-boys holiday in Magaluf in 1999 my mate, Keato, managed to pull a nice-looking girl, and took her back to the apartment. In the morning we piled into his room for the lowdown on his night of action. 'Did you get some, then?' I demanded. 'Yep,' he replied, 'and she clearly loved every minute of it as she's left me a souvenir.' He then disappeared into the bedroom and returned with a pair of yellow knickers. 'Smell that, lads, it's the sweet smell of pussy!' he gloated. And then Dave announced, 'Actually, they're my dirty pants.'